RUBANK EDUCATIONAL LIBRARY

AF796902

RUBANK INTERMEDIATE Method

FLUTE
or PICCOLO

J. E. SKORNICKA and A. C. PETERSEN

A FOLLOW UP COURSE FOR INDIVIDUAL OR LIKE-INSTRUMENT CLASS INSTRUCTION

RUBANK, INC.
MIAMI, FLORIDA

ESSENTIAL PRINCIPLES
of
Good Instrumental Performance

GOOD TONE is necessary in order that one's playing be pleasing to the listener as well as the player. Good tone can be produced only when the instrument is in good playing condition, equipped with the correct type of mouthpiece and played with the correct embouchure.

INTONATION: When two successive tones of different pitch are produced, it is necessary that each tone be in tune with the other, relative to the interval being played.

TUNE: The player must develop and train his ear so that a difference of pitch can be distinguished when playing with others.

NOTE VALUES: The player must develop a rhythmic sense so as to give proper value to tones as represented by the written notes.

BREATHING AND PHRASING: Each is usually dependent on the other. Since teachers of wind instruments differ on the methods of breathing, no special method is advocated, but it soon becomes evident to all players that in order to get good musical phrasing, it is necessary to breathe properly and in the proper places of a composition. It will be to the pupil's advantage to spend much time and effort on this phase of playing and take seriously all suggestions given by the teacher.

EXPRESSION MARKS: Expression marks in music are considered just as important as punctuation in prose and poetry. Good phrasing is the performance of music that has been properly punctuated. Expression marks put character into a mass of notes and if properly observed, will produce satisfying musical effects.

RELAXATION AND PROPER POSITION OF BODY AND HANDS: Whether playing in standing or sitting position, it is necessary that the body be erect and relaxed. Relaxation is the secret to the accomplishment of success in many other professions and trades. The arms must be relaxed, the elbows away from the body and the hands assuming a restful position on the instrument.

SUFFICIENT TIME FOR PRACTICE: Since different pupils require different types and lengths of practice periods, the objective that every pupil should establish is: "I will master the assigned task whether it takes ½ or 2 hours." The accomplishment of a task is far more important than the time that it consumes.

PROPER CARE OF THE INSTRUMENT: Carelessness in the handling of an instrument is the most prevalent handicap to the progress of young players. No pupil can expect to produce good results if the instrument is in poor playing condition. The instrument must be handled carefully and when a disorder is discovered, have it remedied immediately. Constant attention as to the condition of an instrument will pay dividends in the end.

MENTAL ATTITUDE OF TEACHER AND PUPIL: In order that the musical results be satisfactory, both the pupil and teacher must be interested in their task, and must have a perfect understanding of what that task is. The teacher must understand the learning capacities of the pupil so that the pupil in turn will get the type and amount of instruction that he will understand and be able to master.

J. E. S.

REVIEW LESSON

1. Teacher should see to it that the instrument is in good mechanical condition, namely, springs, pads and keys.

2. Rhythms in this lesson are fundamental, and it is expected that the player will have had sufficient experience on the instrument to be able to read the succeeding sections at sight.

3. Rests are just as important as notes, and therefore it is important to have a sound rhythmic conception in order to play well at sight.

4. Attention should be given the embouchre at this time, so that a good tone is produced at all times. Any variation in the embouchre that produces good results must be discovered by both the teacher and pupil.

1

2

3

4

5

Copyright MCMXXXIX by Rubank Inc., Chicago, Ill.
Copyright Renewed
International Copyright Secured

MARKS OF EXPRESSION AND THEIR USE

Pianissimo	*pp*	Very soft	**Fortissimo**	*ff*	Very loud
Piano	*p*	Soft	**Forte**	*f*	Loud
Mezzo Piano	*mp*	Medium soft	**Mezzo forte**	*mf*	Medium loud (Normal tone)

In playing a tone on the flute (unless otherwise marked) the tone should be held at the same level of volume, without increasing or diminishing the volume of sound. This type of a tone will be indicated by means of parellel lines, thus: ═══════

The distance between the parellel lines will signify the difference of volume to be used.
Thus: *pp* ═══ *p* ═══ *mp* ═══ *mf* ═══ *f* ═══ *ff* ═══

1 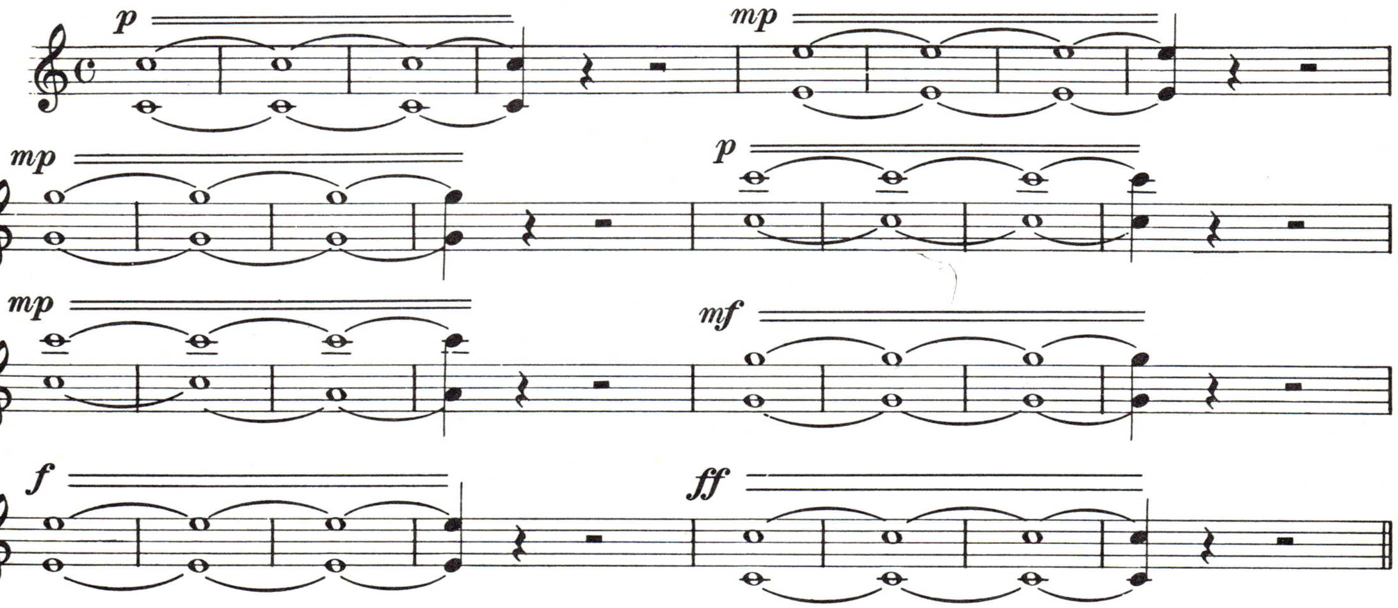

HARMONY

2 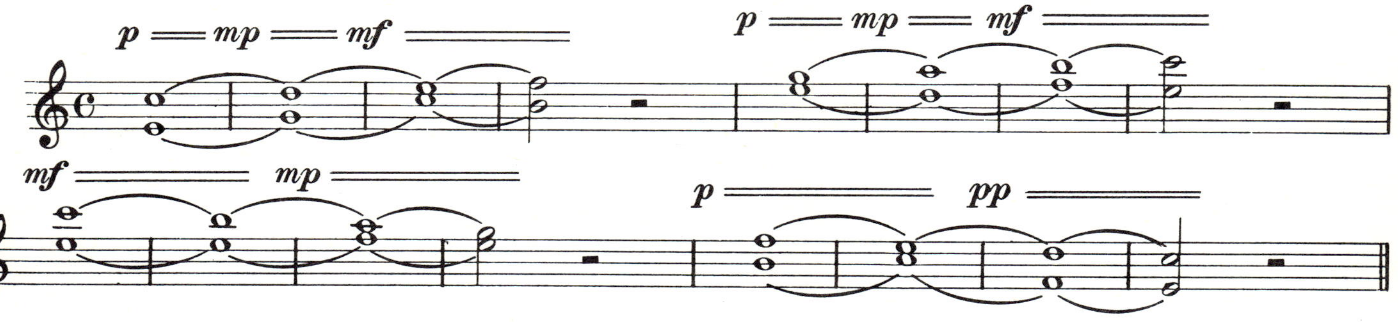

3 

STUDIES IN EXPRESSION

Sound Graduations

Crescendo (cresc.) Gradually louder   Decrescendo (decresc.) or Diminuendo (dim.) Gradually softer

In playing a crescendo or a diminuendo the pitch of the tone should not change. It is a common fault of especially young players, to play flat when playing loud and sharp when playing softly.

In order to play the sound graduations or nuances correctly, it is necessary that the quality of the tone is not affected, but retain its rich and mellow fullness. ONLY THE VOLUME SHOULD CHANGE.

1
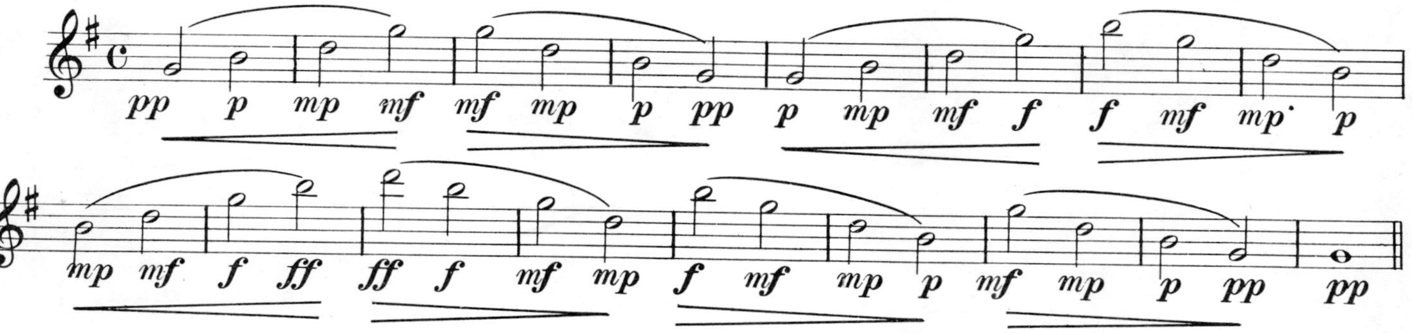

When a note is followed by one or more shorter notes, the shorter notes are played with one half the volume of the longer note. There are exceptions to this rule, but it is a good policy to learn to play all phrases as mentioned, since the majority of all music played in this way will be properly performed. Players interested in the fundamentals of solo playing will be greatly aided by adhering to this principle.

2

3

Using lines 2 and 3 as patterns, write in the various volumes required in the playing of the succeeding song. This will acquaint the player thoroughly with the sound graduations required in the proper performance of solos and songs.

BLUE BELLS OF SCOTLAND

Andante

4

EXPRESSION ETUDES

Tone - Lift flute up. Draw the sides of your lips in for a rounder hole. Play slowly.

DAILY STUDIES FOR THE DEVELOPMENT OF TECHNIC

The studies on this page are intended for daily home practice. These studies, if practiced diligently, will develope a clean and fluent technic. Most of the awkward intervals in the key of C major are included and every finger gets the opportunity to develop independence of action.

Play each study with a steady tempo, slowly at first, but increase the tempo each day until every study on this page can be played fast or Allegro.

Breathe as indicated by the commas, whether you need to or not. Breath marks may be skipped if two complete phrases can be played in one breath.

1

2

3

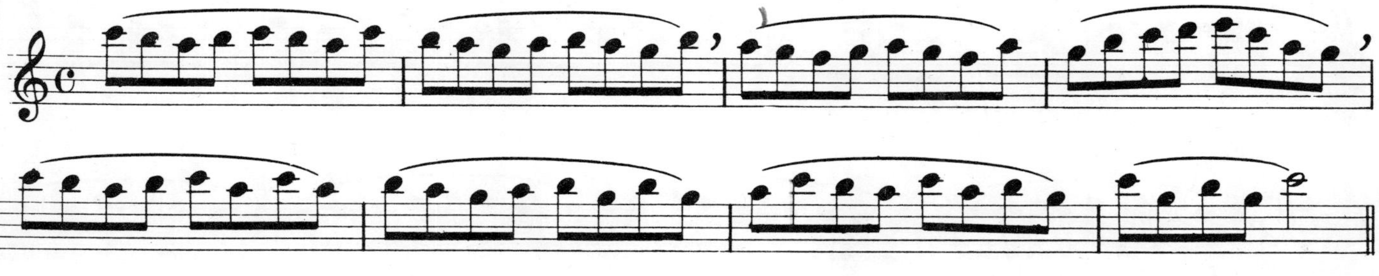

Also play 8va.

4

5

STUDIES IN G MAJOR

G MAJOR CHORD

1

G MAJOR SCALE

2

The use of the F♯.

3

4

5

SUMMER EVENING

Reverie

J. E. S.

STACCATO STUDIES

STACCATO ETUDE

MELODY

PETITE MINUET

ARTICULATION ETUDES

Allegro

1

Moderato

2

Play above Etude with each of the following articulations.

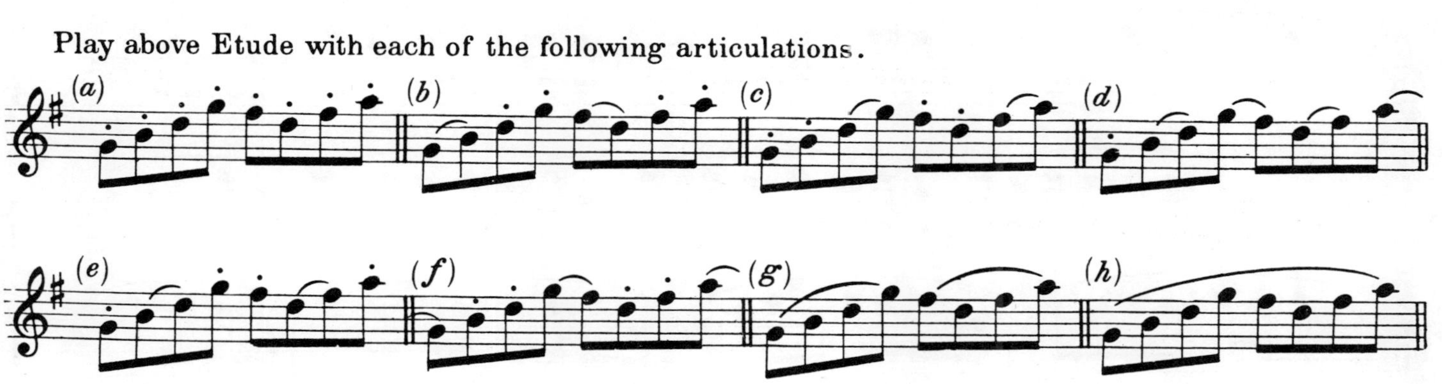

F MAJOR STUDIES

F MAJOR CHORD

1 

F MAJOR SCALE

2 

COUNTRY DANCE

Allegro

3 

TECHNICAL ETUDES

4 

5 

6 

ACCENTS (Rinforzando)

The rinforzando or accent (>) is placed over a note for the purpose of bringing out that particular tone more strongly than the other tones in the same sequence. The rinforzando or accent punctuates the important notes of a measure or sequence.

WALTZ

Moderato

MARCH

Allegro

WOODEN SHOE DANCE

Moderato

SYNCOPATION

The longer note of each measure is to be accented.

1

2

3

SYNCOPATED MELODY

Allegro

4

SYNCOPATION IN 3/4 TIME

Moderato

5

6/8 RHYTHM

Count 6 beats in each measure

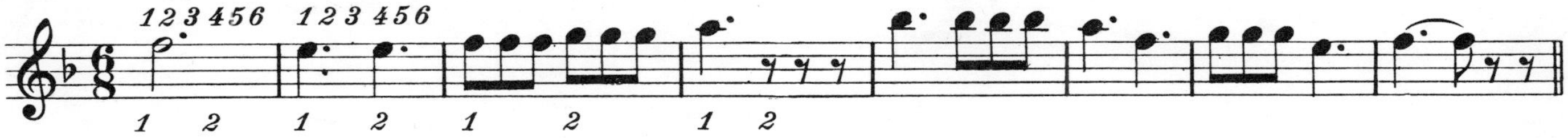

Also count 2 beats in each measure.

6/8 ETUDE

Moderato

MELODY

Allegro

D MINOR (*Melodic*)

D MINOR (*Harmonic*)

B♭ MAJOR STUDIES

B♭ MAJOR CHORD

B♭ MAJOR SCALE

ETUDE IN THIRDS

TECHNICAL ETUDE

MAJOR AND MINOR KEYS IN THIRDS

C MAJOR in Thirds

A MINOR (*Melodic*) in Thirds

A MINOR (*Harmonic*) in Thirds

G MAJOR in Thirds

E MINOR (*Melodic*)

E MINOR (*Harmonic*)

TRIPLET STUDIES

Example

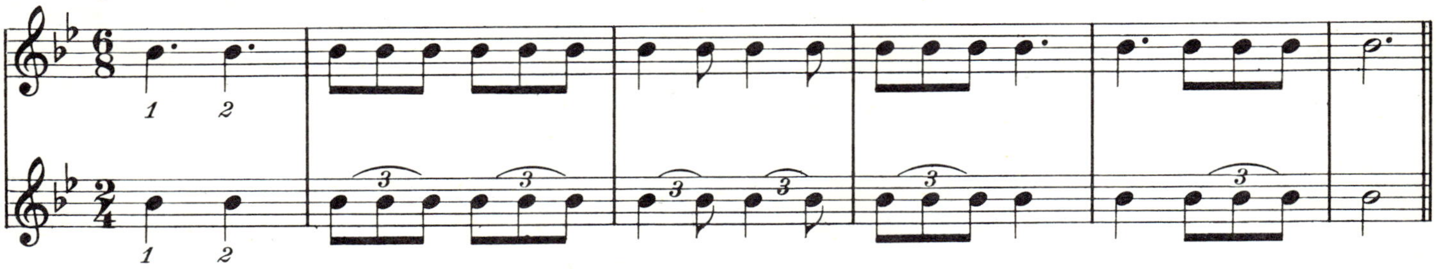

ETUDE IN 6/8 RHYTHM

SAME ETUDE IN 2/4 RHYTHM

G MINOR (*Melodic*)

G MINOR (*Harmonic*)

ARTICULATION STUDIES

FOLK DANCE No. 1

Moderato

FOLK DANCE No. 2

Moderato

STACCATO DUET

Moderato

J. E. S.

D MAJOR STUDIES

D MAJOR CHORD

1

D MAJOR SCALE

2

DAILY STUDIES FOR THE DEVELOPMENT OF TECHNIC

3

4

ETUDE IN D MAJOR

Moderato

WOHLFAHRT

5

DOTTED EIGHTH NOTE STUDIES

Dotted eighth note patterns.

DOTTED EIGHTH NOTE ETUDE

MAZURKA

J. E. S.

B MINOR (*Melodic*)

B MINOR (*Harmonic*)

MAJOR AND MINOR KEYS IN THIRDS

D MAJOR in Thirds

B MINOR (*Melodic*)

B MINOR (*Harmonic*)

F MAJOR in Thirds

5

D MINOR (*Melodic*) in Thirds

6

D MINOR (*Harmonic*) in Thirds

7

E♭ MAJOR STUDIES

E♭ MAJOR CHORD

E♭ MAJOR SCALE

TECHNICAL ETUDE

Moderato

GAVOTTE

Moderato

SHARPSHOOTERS' MARCH

METALO

MAJOR AND MINOR KEYS IN THIRDS

B♭ MAJOR in Thirds

G MINOR (*Melodic*)

G MINOR (*Harmonic*)

E♭ MAJOR in Thirds

C MINOR (*Melodic*)

C MINOR (*Harmonic*)

A MAJOR STUDIES

A MAJOR CHORD

A MAJOR SCALE

TECHNICAL ETUDE IN A MAJOR

Allegro

3

LEGATO STUDY

Moderato Also play 8va

EXERCISING THE TONGUE

Allegro

CHROMATIC STUDIES

2/4 Time

Moderato

1

6/8 Time

Andante

2

2/4 Time

Moderato

3

2/4 Time

Moderato

4

ETUDE

Moderato

5

A♭ MAJOR STUDIES

A♭ MAJOR CHORD

1

A♭ MAJOR SCALE

2

LEGATO STUDY

Moderato

3

GAVOTTE IN A♭

Moderato

4

MAJOR AND MINOR KEYS IN THIRDS

A♭ MAJOR in Thirds

F MINOR (*Melodic*)

F MINOR (*Harmonic*)

A MAJOR in Thirds

F♯ MINOR (*Melodic*)

F♯ MINOR (*Harmonic*)

GRACE NOTES

There are two kinds of Grace notes, short and long. The long grace note acquires half the value of the note that it accompanies, and is seldom used, since it is easy to write out two notes of equal length. The short grace note is the one that is commonly used and will be used in succeeding studies.

In addition to the single grace notes there are double and triple grace notes, but these are usually written out and played on or before the beat. As to which one it shall be is usually determined by the type of music being performed.

SINGLE GRACE NOTES

1

DOUBLE AND TRIPLE GRACE NOTES

2

SINGLE GRACE NOTE ETUDE

3

DOUBLE GRACE NOTES

4

TRIPLE GRACE NOTES

5

Grace Note Etudes

TEMPO DI MINUET

DOUBLE GRACE NOTE ETUDE

TRIPLE GRACE NOTE ETUDE

ABBREVIATIONS

1

2
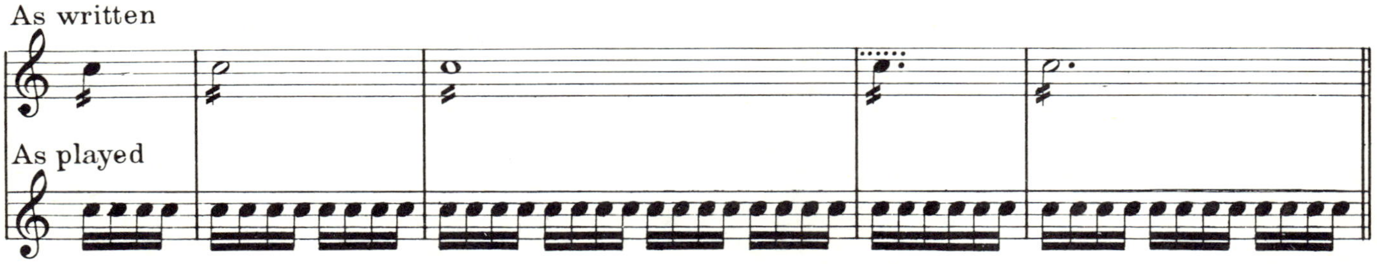

ABBREVIATION STUDIES

3

4

5

6
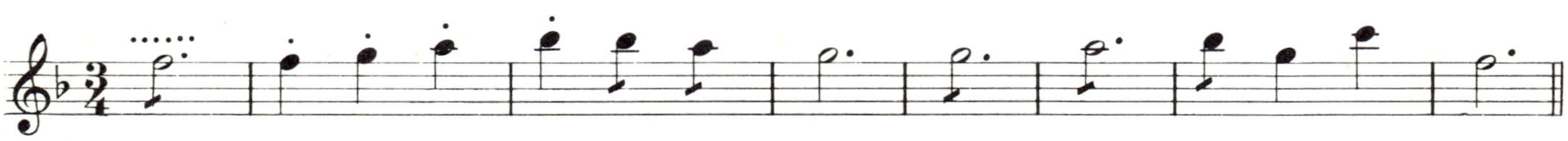

7

POLKA

8

GYPSY POLKA

Allegro

Bohemian

E MAJOR STUDIES

E MAJOR CHORD

E MAJOR SCALE

TECHNICAL ETUDE

THEN YOU'LL REMEMBER ME

DOUBLE TONGUEING

Double tongueing is usually applied in very rapid passages only. This articulation consists of two strokes of the tongue, one forward on the letter T, and one backwards on the letter K. It is necessary that both of these strokes be practiced well so that a good tone is produced on both strokes.

1

2

3

SCALE AND CHORD ETUDE

4

ARTICULATION ETUDE

5

SYNCHRONIZING THE FINGERS AND TONGUE

6

CHORD ETUDE

CHROMATIC ETUDE

LAENDLER

KMOCH

THE GRUPETTO OR TURN (∾)

1

2

ETUDE

3

4

ETUDE

5

TRIPLE TONGUEING

Like double tongueing, triple tongueing is applied to very fast passages only. The tongue has to make three (3) strokes and are produced by using the three letters T K T. The player must be carefull to produce equal tones on each of the letters.

1

2

3

4

USING 5th AND 6th FINGERS

The 6th finger is most commonly used, however, the 5th is used in rapid passages.

1

E MAJOR in Thirds

C# MINOR (*Melodic*)

C# MINOR (*Harmonic*)

TRILLS

A trill is produced by alternating the given or written tone and the next scale tone above in rapid succession. As an example, if the given or written tone to be trilled is E and the key being played is the key of C major, the scale tone above will be F natural. If, however, the key being played is G major, the next scale tone above E will be F♯. In the first instant, the trill will alternate between E and F natural and in the second instant, between E and F♯.

The approximate number of notes usually played on a trilled tone is shown below. The same number of tones is not always played, because on long tones, the trill starts slowly and accelerates in rapidity to the end of that tone, however the examples below show the exact number of notes in a regular trill.

On long tones or tones of a slow passage a trill is usually closed with an additional tone which is the tone directly below the given or written tone. The closing tone is not usually used when playing a short trill or a trill in a fast passage.

Sometimes it is necessary to alter the pitch of the closing tone, and this is done by indicating thus: (tr♯) (tr♮)(tr♭). The key in which the trill appears, determines which one of three symbols is to be used, however the purpose of these symbols is the same, namely, to have the closing tone either a half step or whole step from the given or written tone. When the sharp, flat or the natural appear above the trill thus: (♯tr) (♮tr)(♭tr), it is an indication that the tone above the given or written tone may have its pitch altered to fit the key or modulation intended in the music being performed.

When the closing tones of a trill are to be emphasized and ritarded, these two tones are usually written out to insure their being played. This is especially done on long tones or holds which end a phrase or a cadenza.

TRILL CHART FOR BOEHM SYSTEM FLUTE

Where more than one fingering is listed for the same trill, the first is preferred, although the second may be more effective on some flutes.

1. The numbers,(1-2-3-4-5-6-), indicate the 6 large fingers of both hands.
2. (B♭-B), Left hand thumb, (X) indicates when used.
3. (G♯), Left hand little finger, (X) indicates when used.
4. (D♯), Right hand little finger, (X) indicates when used.
5. (◯), Circle around number or key name, indicates the keys in motion in the production of the trill.
6. Trill keys, upper and lower, (X) indicates when used.

1st	1	1	1	1 1	1	1	1	1	1 1	1	1	1	1	1 1	1	1
B♭														× ×	×	
B♮	×	×	×	× ×	×	×	×	×	× ×	×	×	×	×			×
2nd	2	2	2	2 2	2	2	2	2	2 2	2	2	2	2	② ②	②	②
3rd	3	3	3	3 3	3	3	3	3	3 3	3	3	③	③③	③ 3		
G♯										ⓧ	ⓧ		× ⓧ	× ×		
				or					or				or	or		
4th	4	4	4	4 4	4	④	④	④								
Trill key																
5th	5	5	5	⑤⑤	⑤	5			⑤							
Trill key																
6th	6	⑥	⑥	⑥ 6			6		⑥	6						
D♯	ⓧ		×	× ×	×	×	×	×	× ×	×	×	×	× ×	× ×	×	×

1st	1	1 1	1	①	①	1											
B♭		ⓧ															
B♮	×	ⓧ	ⓧ	ⓧ					×	×	×	× ×	×	×	×	×	× ×
2nd									2	2	2	2 2	2	2	2	2	2 2
3rd									3	3	3	3 3	3	3	3	3	3 3
G♯																	
		or										or					or
4th	④	4							4	4	4	4 4	4	④	④	④	
Trill key						ⓧ	ⓧ										
5th									5	5	5	⑤⑤	⑤	5			⑤
Trill key								ⓧ									
6th									6	⑥	⑥	⑥ 6			6		⑥
D♯	×	× ×	×	×	×	×			ⓧ		×	× ×	×	×	×	×	× ×

	1	2	3	4	5	6	7	8	9	10	11	12	13	14	15	16
1st	1	1	1	1 1	1 1	1	1	1	1 1	1	①	①	1			
B♭					× ×	×			⊗							
B♮	×	×	×	× ×			×	×	⊗	⊗	⊗					×
2nd	2	2	2	2 2	②②	②	②									2
3rd	3	3	③	③③	③ 3											3
G♯	⊗	⊗		× ⊗	× ×											⊗
				or	or				or							
4th								④	4							
Trill key														⊗	⊗	
5th																
Trill key													⊗		⊗	
6th	6															
D♯	×	×	×	× ×	× ×	×	×	×	× ×	×	×	×	×	×	×	×

	1	2	3	4	5	6	7	8	9	10	11	12	13	14	15	16	17
1st			1 1	1	1 1	1	1	1 1	①	① 1					1	1	1
B♭																	
B♮	×	×	× ×	×	⊗ ×	×	⊗	⊗⊗	⊗		×			×	×	×	⊗
2nd	2	2	②②	②	2 ②					2 2	2	2	2	②	②		
3rd	③	③	③ 3			3	3	3 3	3	3 3	③	3	3		3	3	3
G♯		⊗	⊗ ×									×	×				
			or		or					or							
4th		4	4 4	4	4	④	4							4	④	④	
Trill key										⊗		⊗	⊗			⊗	
5th		5	5 5	5	5			5			5						
Trill key													⊗				×
6th		6	6 6			6		6	6		6				6		
D♯	×	×	× ×	×	× ×	×	×	× ×	×	×	×	×	×	×			

LEGATO TRILL ETUDE

1

STACCATO TRILL ETUDE

2

6/8 STUDY

ARTICULATION STUDY

TWO-PART INVENTION

BACH

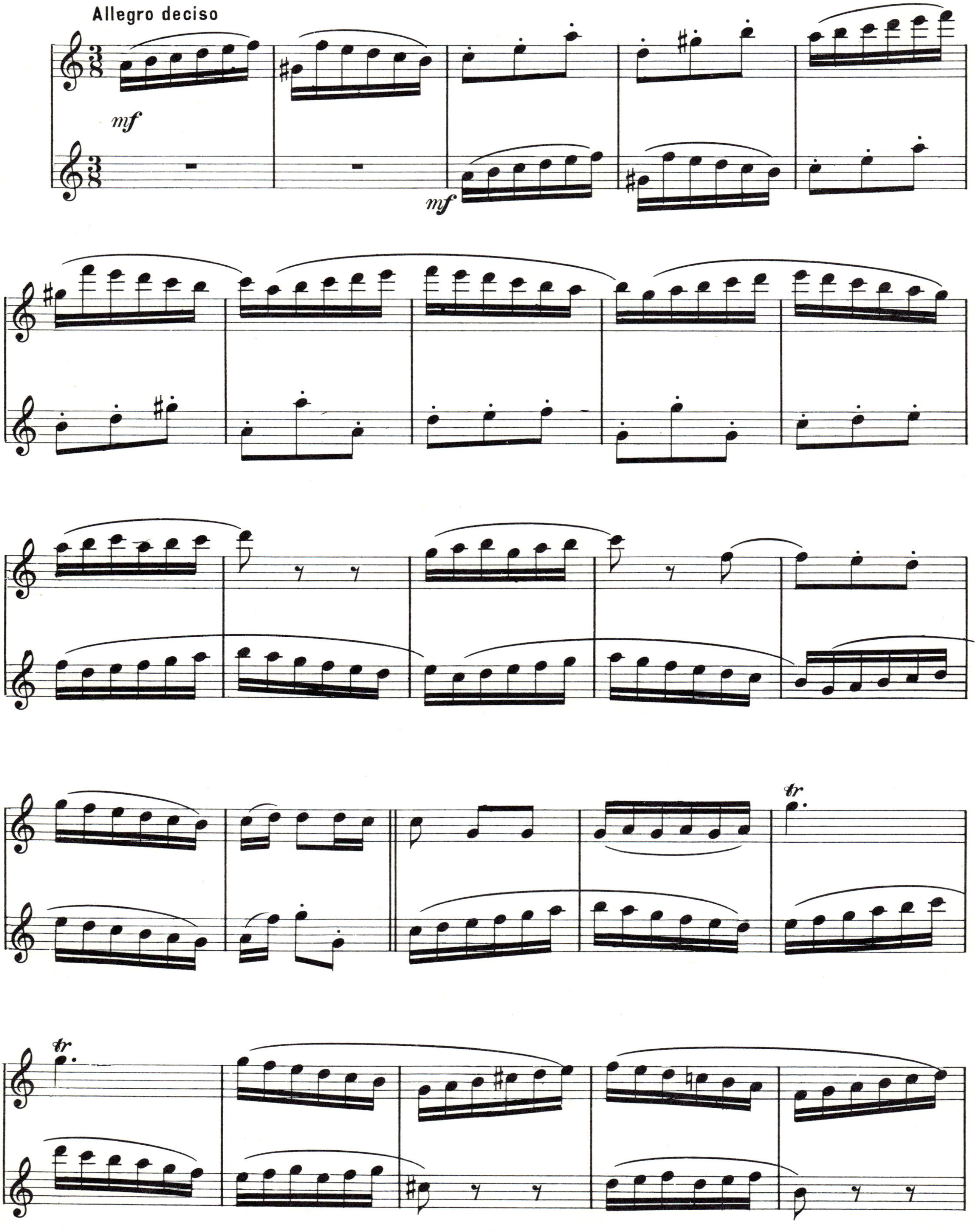

rit.

DUET BRILLIANT

Allegro

J.E.S.